LOOKING OUT THE WINDOW

By Azriel Bin Omar

Library For All Ltd.

Looking out the Window

First published 2023

Published by Library For All Ltd
Email: info@libraryforall.org
URL: libraryforall.org

Our Yarning logo design by Jason Lee, Bidjipidji Art

Original illustrations by Meg Turner

Looking out the Window
Bin Omar, Azriel
ISBN: 978-1-922991-91-1
SKU03381

LOOKING OUT THE WINDOW

We respect and honour Aboriginal and Torres Strait Islander Elders past, present and future. We acknowledge the stories, traditions and living cultures of Aboriginal and Torres Strait Islander peoples on this land and commit to building a brighter future together.

Driving home to Derby with mum, Faith was bored.

"I'm bored," she said to her mum. "What can we do?"

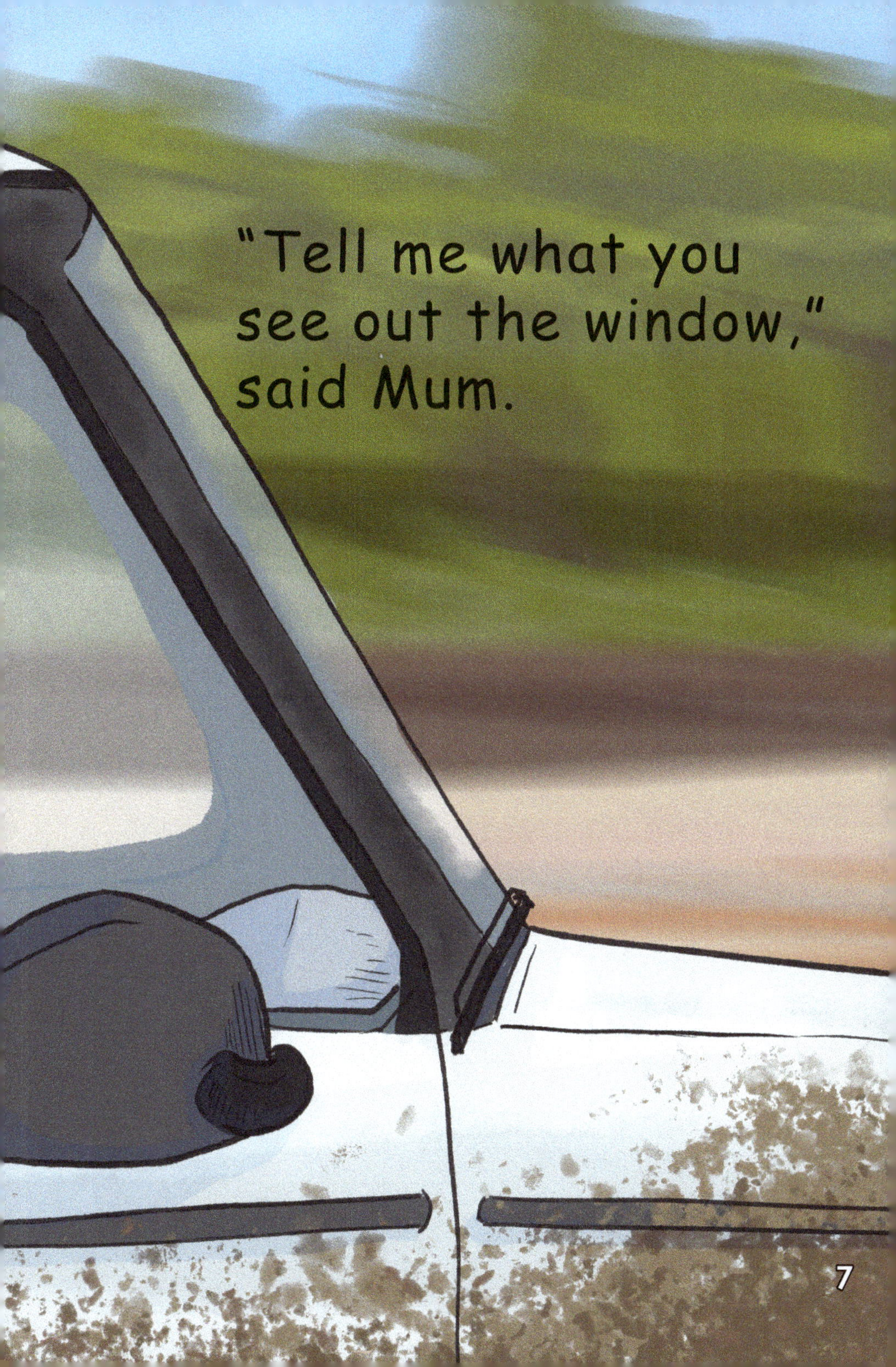

"Tell me what you see out the window," said Mum.

"Hmmm, out the window, I see a lot of tall green trees with white cockatoos in them."

"What else can you see?"
asked Mum.

"I can see brown muddy waters as we go across the bridge."

"I can see a roadhouse with lots of crows everywhere," said Mum.

"I see it, too!" said Faith.

"Yay! We are almost home," Faith said.

The trip goes much faster when you look out the window.

Soon, big beautiful Boab trees were everywhere and Faith was home.

You can use these questions to talk about this book with your family, friends and teachers.

What did you learn from this book?

Describe this book in one word. Funny? Scary? Colourful? Interesting?

How did this book make you feel when you finished reading it?

What was your favourite part of this book?

About the contributors

Azriel was born in Broome and lives in Derby. She enjoys fishing and throwing the net with her dad in the river. When she was younger, she loved reading *Where is Nana?*.

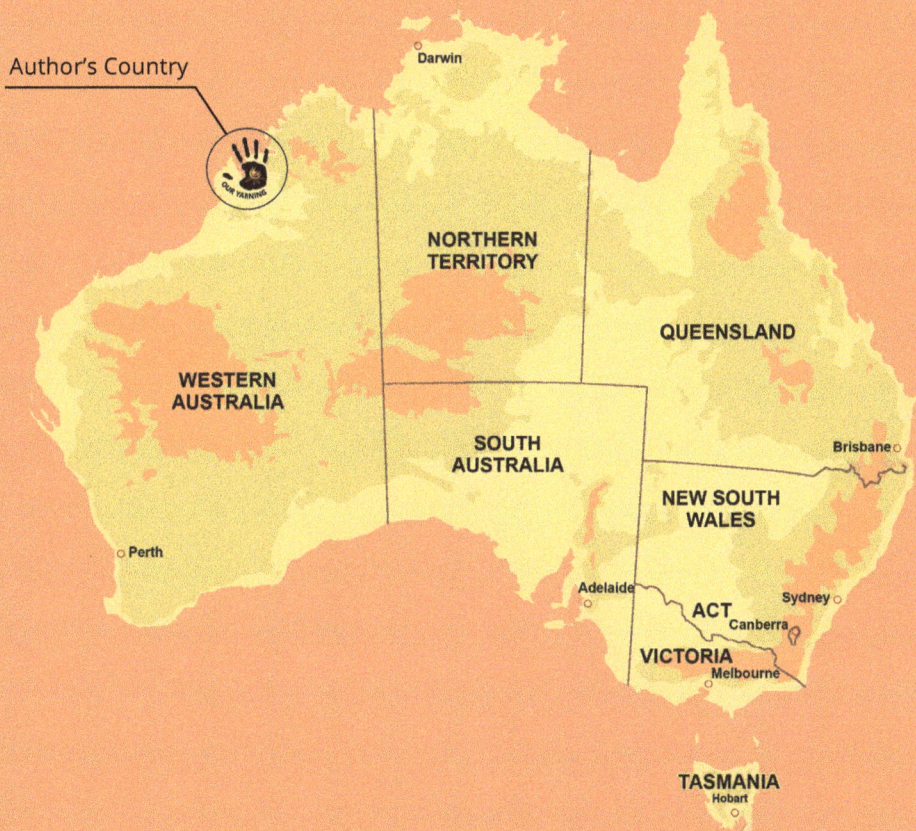

Author's Country

Darwin

OUR YARNING

NORTHERN
TERRITORY

QUEENSLAND

WESTERN
AUSTRALIA

SOUTH
AUSTRALIA

Brisbane

NEW SOUTH
WALES

Perth

Adelaide

Sydney

ACT
Canberra

VICTORIA
Melbourne

TASMANIA
Hobart

Our Yarning

Want to discover more books from this collection? Our Yarning is a collection of books written by Aboriginal and Torres Strait Islander peoples across Australia.

We know that children learn better, and enjoy reading more, when they see themselves in the stories, characters and illustrations of the books they read.

To download the app, visit the Google Play Store on any Android device and search 'Our Yarning'.